Harriet Adams Sawyer, A. B. Greene

A Song of the Christ

Harriet Adams Sawyer, A. B. Greene

A Song of the Christ

ISBN/EAN: 9783337181383

Printed in Europe, USA, Canada, Australia, Japan

Cover: Foto ©Thomas Meinert / pixelio.de

More available books at **www.hansebooks.com**

See the sick unto Him fleeing,
    Bounteous healing to receive;
See the blind their dark way groping,
    As He bids them look and live.

BY

HARRIET ADAMS SAWYER

ILLUSTRATED WITH SIXTEEN FULL-PAGE PLATES

BY A. B. GREENE

BOSTON

D. LOTHROP COMPANY

1893

"IT IS I, BE NOT AFRAID."

CONTENTS.

LIST OF ILLUSTRATIONS.

THE STAR OF BETHLEHEM

THE STAR OF BETHLEHEM.

O. holy Star. down through the darkness
  gleaming
  On shepherds watching o'er their flocks
  by night.
Tell them thy gentle radiance softly streaming
  Shall fill the saddened earth with peace
  and light.

O. tell them that new-born. that heavenly
  Stranger.
  By Virgin-Mother watched in wondering
  love —
That beauteous Babe. lying in Bethlehem's
  manger —
  Is Israel's Shepherd. promised from
  above.

Fear not, O wondering shepherds! hear the
    singing
  Borne on the night wind by the angel's
    voice ;
In rapturous strains the joyful tidings
    bringing,
  The Christ is born ! Let Heaven and
    earth rejoice !

O, light ineffable ! O, music swelling !
  Angelic choristers their voices raise —
" Glory to God on high," their rapture
    telling.
  " Peace and good-will toward men," their
    song of praise

O, holy Star, down through the darkness gleaming
    On shepherds watching o'er their flocks by night,
Tell them thy gentle radiance softly streaming
    Shall fill the saddened earth with peace and light.

CHILDREN'S
SONG OF CHRIST'S BIRTH

ANGELS SALUTED THE HEAVENLY STRANGER.

.

CHILDREN'S SONG OF CHRIST'S BIRTH.

Hail to the Infant that lay in the manger.
   So sang the shepherds, so sing we to-day.
Angels saluted the heavenly Stranger.
   Still will He welcome the homage we pay.

Hail! blessed Jesus, the Friend of the
      children;
  " Suffer them," said He, " to come unto
     me,"
Folding them tenderly unto His bosom;
   Men stand in wonder and awe, as they see.

Our heart's truest service we joyfully
render.
Who shall forbid us, when Jesus says
" Come ? "
Praises of children are sweet to the Saviour,
He said, that of such is His heavenly
Home.

Hosanna! Hosanna! we sing unto Jesus,
In Bethlehem born for our Saviour and
King ;
We'll love Him, and serve Him, and praise
Him forever,
Accept now, dear Jesus, the tribute we
bring.

" WHO SHALL FORBID US, WHEN JESUS SAYS ' COME? ' "

Opening Heaven tells his birthright,
That the people may believe.

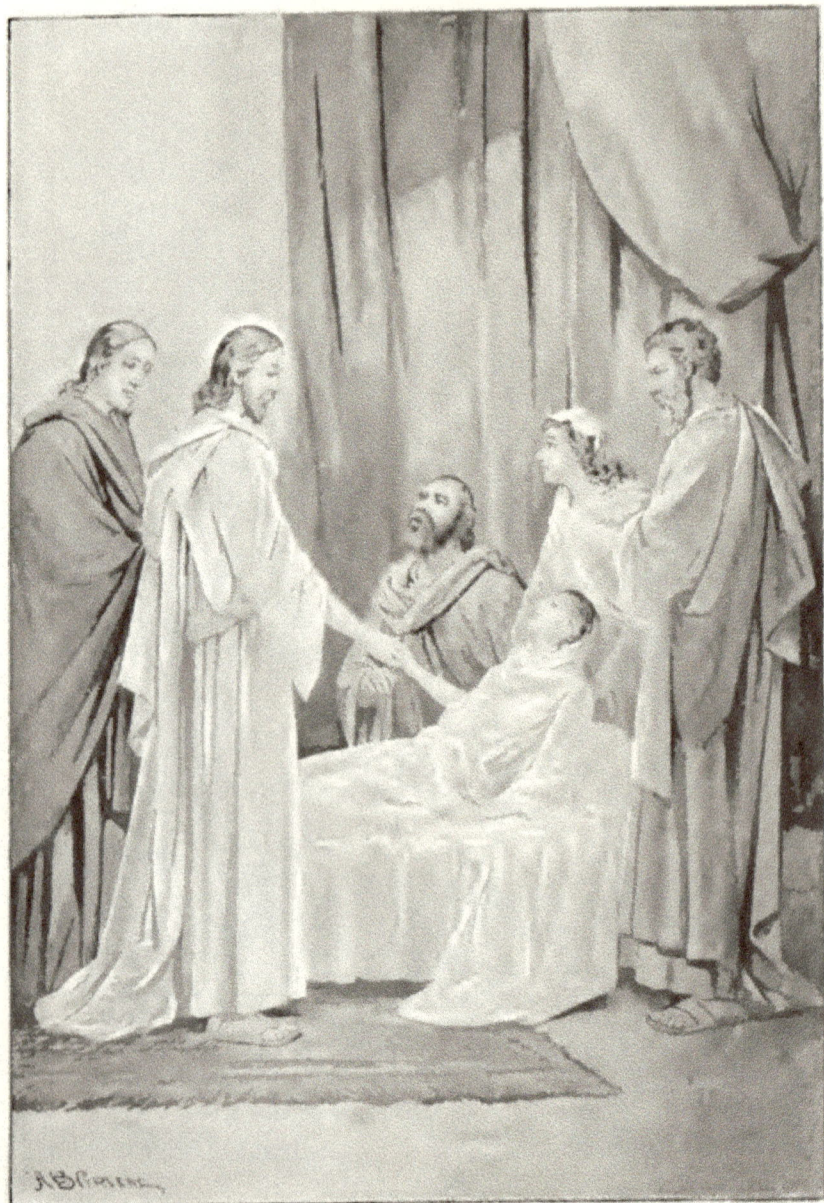

See the dead come forth exulting
From the darkness of the grave.

CHRIST'S MISSION

Who this Stranger strong and kingly,
Who this holy Nazarene?

CHRIST'S MISSION.

Who this Stranger strong and kingly,
   Who this holy Nazarene?
Ne'er such wonders men have witnessed,
   Ne'er such tenderness was seen.

On the bank of Jordan standing,
   Holy baptism to receive,
Opening Heaven tells His birthright,
   That the people may believe.

God's own voice is heard attesting,
   " This is my beloved Son,"
While the light of Heaven rested
   Like a dove, His form upon.

See the sick unto Him fleeing,
  Bounteous healing to receive;
See the blind their dark way groping,
  As He bids them look and live.

See the tempest wildly raging,
  Hear Him saying, " Peace, be still!"
Waves their restless fury ceasing,
  Bow, obedient to His will.

See the dead come forth exulting,
  From the darkness of the grave;
See the devils shrink from mortals
  Ransomed by His power to save.

See the woman touch His garment,
    As He walks His Holy way.
" Daughter, now thy faith hath saved thee ;
    Go in peace," Oh! hear Him say.

See the tempest wildly raging,
Hear Him saying, "Peace, be still!"

See the woman touch His garment.
  As He walks His holy way.
" Daughter. now thy faith hath saved thee.
  Go in peace." Oh! hear Him say.

See Him walk upon the water ;
  His disciples. filled with dread.
Hear in joy His gentle accents.
  " It is I. be not afraid."

See the deaf. the lame. the leprous.
  Finding healing. strength and rest.
See the sinner. heavy laden.
  Go forgiven. saved and blest

When the multitude had waited
  Days and nights upon His word;
Without food had lingered near Him,
  His divine compassion stirred.

By His power He fed the thousands
  From a small and scanty store:
And when all were filled and strengthened,
  There was still enough for more.

To the tale of human sorrow
  Never turned He yet away.
This the Saviour whom we worship
  In our songs this Christmas Day.

See the sinner, heavy-laden,
Go forgiven, saved and blest

By his power He fed the thousands
From a small and scanty store.

THE CRUCIFIXION

THE CRUCIFIXION.

He dies! He dies on Calvary.
   The spotless Lamb of God —
He pays with His own precious blood
   Our debt — the fearful load.

The cruel spear, the crown of thorns.
   The taunt of angry men.
Are borne, that we may never bear
   The curse and gloom again.

The hand that only moved to bless
   Is pierced by those it blessed.
That hungry souls may look and live.
   And all the weary rest.

" Father, forgive them," hear Him cry;
   " They know not what they do."
He bows His sacred head, and dies.
   High Heaven beholds the view.

The cruel work is done at last;
   "'Tis finished," hear Him cry.
But Heaven frowns that God's own Son
   Upon the cross should die.

The earth doth quake — the rocks are rent,
  The graves yield up their dead —
'Tis darkness over all the land;
  The people are afraid.

The earth doth quake — the rocks are rent.
　The graves yield up their dead —
'Tis darkness over all the land ;
　The people are afraid.

Redemption's work is surely done.
　The wine-press He hath trod —
The wondering people say. at length.
　" This was the Son of God."

CHILDREN'S SONG
OF THE RESURRECTION

CHILDREN'S SONG OF THE RESURRECTION.

The body was wrapped in linen white,
And borne by loving hands at night
To Joseph's tomb, ne'er used before,
And a great stone rolled 'gainst the door.

His enemies feared that His words prove
    true,
So they sealed the stone, and set watchers,
    too ;
They said, " His disciples will come by
    night,
And steal Him away from our care and
    sight."

But the stone and the watchmen were all in
      vain.
The Saviour had said He would rise again,
And when was come the appointed hour,
He burst the bands of death with power.

The angel descended at break of day
And rolled the stone from the door away —
His raiment was white as the new fall'n
      snow,
And his face had the lightning's vivid glow.

And unto the women the angel said:
"Why seek ye the living among the dead?"
The listening watchmen, filled with fear,
Hear the angel say, "He is not here;

And unto the women the angel said:
" Why seek ye the living among the dead? "

. . . .

" The Lord is risen; be not afraid,
But come and see where His form was laid;
Then go your way the glad news to tell
To disciples and friends He loved so well."

" The Lord is risen ; be not afraid,
But come and see where His form was laid ;
Then go your way the glad news to tell
To disciples and friends He loved so well."

Then hastening on in joy and fear,
" All hail !" said Jesus, drawing near —
Once more their loving Lord they greet,
And bowing, worship at His feet.

His last command they now receive :
" Go teach all nations to believe,
You as my witnesses I send,
Lo ! I am with you to the end."

ON THE WAY TO EMMAUS

ON THE WAY TO EMMAUS.

On Emmaus' road when walking on that
    day,
Two sad disciples met Him by the way;
In tenderness He taught them of the Word.
But they wist not their teacher was their
    Lord.

Thus they constrained Him. " It is even-
    tide.
For spent the day is — then with us abide,"
And as He blessed and brake the bread
    that night
They knew Him — and He vanished from
    their sight.

In patient, tender love He taught them still,
How He had come the Scriptures to fulfill;
Showed unto them his pierced hands and
    feet,
And, with His own, their simple fare did
    eat.

And when at last His work on earth was
    o'er —
To Bethany He led them forth once more;
With lifted hands His blessing there was
    given,
Then passed He from them, through the
    clouds, to Heaven.

Two sad disciples met Him by the way;
In tenderness He taught them of the Word,
But they wist not their teacher was their Lord.

JUBILEE

OVER THE FINISHED WORK

JUBILEE OVER THE FINISHED WORK.

Sing, sing, ye people, and shout, shout for
    joy,
For Satan, our foe, Jesus came to destroy,
To our great Deliverer our honors we pay,
Shouting His praises on this Christmas
    Day.

The heathen in darkness are seeing the
    light:
The morning now dawns after blackness of
    night:
The idols are falling, and, hearing the
    word,
The nations are putting their trust in the
    Lord.

O, give us, dear Saviour, a heart full of
    love!
As Christ, our example, came down from
    above
To rescue the perishing — so may we go,
And tell the glad message till all men shall
    know :

Till the glory of God spreads o'er land and
    o'er sea,
And the whole earth shall join in one glad
    jubilee,
Then praise to the Father, and praise to
    the Son,
And praise to the Spirit, the blest Three in
    One.

Till the glory of God spreads o'er land and o'er sea;
And the whole earth shall join in one glad jubilee.
Then praise to the Father, and praise to the Son,
And praise to the Spirit, the blest Three in One.